The Pecan Tree: A True Friend

Contents

The Pecan Tree: A True Friend

Barbara A. Langham

A Langham Publication
1994

Barbara A. Langham
P.O. Box 162881
Austin, Texas 78716

Layout and design by Alan Kenney

First Edition
10 9 8 7 6 5 4 3 2 1

Library of Congress Cataloging in Publication Data
Langham, Barbara A.
The Pecan Tree: A True Friend
(1. Juvenile literature - nonfiction 2. Horticulture -
pecans 3. Frontier life and history) I. Title.

Library of Congress Catalog Card No. 94-96074
ISBN 0-9640804-0-0

How It Became a State Tree

The day was March 2—Texas Independence Day—and the year was 1906. James Stephen Hogg was visiting a friend in Houston.

Mr. Hogg was a businessman. A few years earlier, from 1891 to 1895, he had been Governor of Texas. On this day, he was not feeling well. He had been hurt in a railroad accident several months before and had never fully healed.

That night, Governor Hogg told his friend, "When I die, I want a pecan tree planted at the head of my grave and a walnut tree at my feet." He wanted the nuts from

1

those trees to be planted everywhere to make Texas a land of trees.

Governor Hogg said good-night and went to bed. Late the next morning, he died in his sleep.

His last wish was granted. The trees were planted at his grave in Oakwood Cemetery in Austin.

When Governor Hogg died, newspapers carried stories about his last wish. People began to take interest in pecan trees.

Instead of cutting them down to make farmland, they let them grow. They began to think of pecan trees as special. In 1919 the Texas Legislature named the pecan the State Tree of Texas.

Today pecan trees grow nearly everywhere in Texas. They grow by the State Capitol in Austin, around many county courthouses, and in many parks.

One Texas town, Seguin, has a pecan monument by its county courthouse. The pecan is made of plaster and is as large as a bicycle.

For many years the pecans from the tree at Governor Hogg's grave were given to school children all over Texas. In 1969 a new pecan tree was planted in place of the old one. It still stands at the grave.

Where is your favorite pecan tree? Is it down the street? Is it in a park? Is it at your Grandpa's and Grandma's house?

Why It's a True Friend

Pecan trees are our good friends. They give us cool shade in the summer and pecans in the fall. They make homes for birds and small animals such as squirrels.

Pecan trees have been our friends for hundreds of years. Native Americans gathered pecans from trees growing wild along rivers and creeks.

Native Americans ate pecans in different ways. They cracked pecans and ate them raw. They roasted pecans and covered them with wild honey. They also ground up the pecans to use in pemmican.

Pemmican was a food much like the granola bars we eat today. To make pemmican, Native Americans would mix pecans with bits of dried buffalo or deer meat, other foods, and fat. Then they would stuff the mixture into a strip of animal intestine. Pemmican lasted a long time and was good for carrying on trips.

The first European to find pecans was Cabeza de Vaca, a Spanish explorer whose ship wrecked off the Gulf Coast in 1528. He called pecans *nueces* (nuts) or *nogales* (walnuts). He saw Native Americans gathering pecans along a river, which may have been the Guadalupe or Colorado River in Texas.

Later other Spanish and French explorers found pecans growing along the Illinois and Mississippi Rivers. By the 1790s, when the United States was still a young country, George Washington and Thomas Jefferson grew pecan trees in their gardens in Virginia.

In the 1800s, as more people moved west, Native Americans showed them that pecans were good to eat. In the 1860s, a German baker, Gustav Duerler, bought pecans to use in his pastries in Texas. By the 1880s he was shipping pecans from San Antonio to many places in the United States.

In 1872, a 19-year-old man from England landed at Galveston. Edmund E. Risien was on his way to California, but he stopped to visit some of his family in Texas.

When he came to San Saba, he had only a little money left. He found a job making furniture. While working, he noticed someone selling the biggest pecans he had ever seen. He found out which tree grew the

pecans and bought the land where it stood. The tree later became known as the "mother" tree because he used it to create more than 20 new varieties of pecans.

In 1888 he started a nursery for selling pecans and budwood. He sold pecans to people in many parts of the United States and the world. One of his most famous customers was Queen Victoria of England.

Every year he invited the school children in San Saba to gather pecans that fell from his trees.

In the early 1900s most people in the South lived on farms. In the fall, children and their families picked pecans. Today many farmers have planted pecan trees in orchards so they can sell the pecans. Today pecan trees grow in Texas, Oklahoma, Arkansas, Louisiana, Mississippi, Alabama, Georgia, and north to Kansas, Missouri, and Tennessee.

Pecans have even gone to the moon. In the early 1970s astronauts on Apollo flights 13, 14, 15, 16, and 17 ate pecans as part of their food while traveling in space. Since pecans are small, they are easy to store on the spacecraft. They don't mind the heat or cold, and they give people lots of energy.

How Pecans Grow

Pecan trees bear nuts once a year. How the nuts grow is an interesting story.

In the winter, pecan trees have no leaves on their limbs. If you listen carefully, you may hear their bare branches rattle in the wind.

In the spring when wildflowers bloom, tiny buds appear on the pecan branches. These buds grow into leaves.

As the leaves come out in April, you will see long, green "fingers" hanging from the stems. These "fingers" are catkins, or male flowers. They make pollen.

The stigmas, or female flowers, may be hard to find. They grow on the ends of new shoots. They are green at first and turn yellow when they are ready to receive pollen. Some types turn red. They have a sticky or velvet surface.

In April and May, the wind blows and shakes the pollen off the catkins. The pollen lands on other pecan trees and sticks to the female flowers. After giving off their pollen, the catkins dry up and fall off. The female flowers then turn into nutlets.

All summer, the pecans grow larger and larger. All you can see are the green shucks on the outside. In August and September, the pecans are filling a sack, which turns into the kernel.

In October the brown shells inside harden, and the green shucks begin to split open. By Halloween, you may see some pecans that have fallen to the ground. Or you can shake the branches to make the pecans fall out of their shucks.

In November and December, the tree's leaves and shucks turn brown, and the pecans fall easily. Once again the tree is empty and ready for a long winter rest.

How We Use Pecans

When pecans begin to drop out of the trees, we have to hurry to gather them. Otherwise, squirrels, crows, and other animals may eat them.

Pecan growers who have lots of trees use machines to gather pecans. First, workers spread canvas on the ground.

They use a machine with long arms to shake the tree and make the pecans fall onto the canvas.

They scoop up the pecans and dump them from the canvas into a trailer.

After sorting out the twigs and leaves, they place the pecans in large bags. They sell some of the bags to grocery stores and take other bags to a shelling plant.

At the shelling plant, the pecans go through machines that crack the nuts and shake out the kernels.

Workers check the kernels carefully and remove any shell pieces. Then they pack the kernels into small bags and sell them to bakeries and shops.

If you have unshelled pecans, you can use a nutcracker to crack them open. Nutcrackers come in all shapes and sizes. The simplest one is shaped like a V. You place a pecan near the point of the V and squeeze the two handles. With practice, you will learn how to crack pecans without crushing the kernel.

Pecans ripen just in time for Thanksgiving and the holidays. We use pecans in sweets such as pecan pie, fruitcake, cookies, and candy. But they also taste good in breads, salads, and other dishes. Many people like to eat them straight from the shell.

Try making these pecan dishes. Make sure an adult is nearby when you are cooking.

Roasted Pecans

You will need:

◆ 1 pound shelled pecans (halves or large pieces)

◆ 1 or 2 tablespoons melted butter or margarine

1. Spread the pecans on an ungreased cookie sheet. Bake for 10 minutes in the oven at 300 degrees Fahrenheit.

2. Stir the pecans with a long wooden spoon so they can roast evenly. Bake for another 10 minutes or until they are crisp. Let the pecans cool. If you like, drizzle them with melted butter.

Mexican Wedding Cookies

You will need:

◆ 1 cup softened butter or margarine

◆ 4 tablespoons powdered sugar

- 2 teaspoons vanilla
- 1 tablespoon cold water
- 2 cups flour
- 1 cup chopped pecans

1. Place the butter and powdered sugar in a large bowl and mix together until creamy.

2. Add the vanilla and water, and mix again.

3. Stir in the flour.

4. Add the pecans and stir well.

5. Empty the batter on a large sheet of waxed paper. With your fingers, shape small amounts of batter into strips about two inches long.

6. Place the strips on an ungreased cookie sheet. Bake in an oven at 300 degrees Fahrenheit for 20 minutes or until light brown.

7. Remove the cookies from the cookie sheet with a flat spatula. While the cookies are still hot, roll them in more powdered sugar.

Pecan Butter

You will need:
- 1 cup shelled pecans
- 1/2 cup butter or margarine

1. Place the butter in a bowl and mash it with a spoon until it is soft and creamy.

2. Chop the pecans in a food chopper until they are in small pieces. Stir the pecans into the butter. Spread the pecan butter on pancakes, waffles, or toast. Store any leftover pecan butter in the refrigerator.

What can you do with the shells from pecans? Some people spread them in flower beds to help break up the soil. Some people use them as kindling in fireplaces and barbecue pits.

Can you think of other ways to use the shells? Try pasting broken shells on paper to make a collage. If you like, use paint or crayons to make a picture.

Play games with pecans. Many years ago when children had few toys, they played with things they found outdoors. One game was "Hully Gully Handful." To play, take a few pecan shells or small native pecans in your hands. Put both your hands behind you where your friends cannot see them. Take two or three pecan shells in one hand, and close your hand in a fist. Show your fist to your friends, and say, "Hully gully handful." When someone guesses how many you are holding, open your fist. Take turns.

# Grow Your Own Pecan Tree

Would you like to grow your own pecan tree?

What do you use as a seed? For a clue, look around under your favorite pecan tree. You may find a young tree that has come up by itself. Where did it come from?

Sometimes when people don't pick up all the pecans, one gets buried in the dirt, and it sprouts. So the nut is the seed. Look at the pecan sprouting in the picture at left.

If you want to grow a tree from seed, find a fresh pecan with a smooth shell that has no stains, splits, or cracks.

In the fall or winter, find a place outdoors that has room for a big tree to grow.

Dig a hole about three inches deep in the dirt, drop the pecan in the hole, and cover it with dirt. Place stones around the hole, or cover it with chicken wire to mark the spot.

If there are squirrels or dogs around, they may dig up your pecan. You may want to plant the pecan in a container and keep it indoors on a sunny window sill. The container can be a five-gallon bucket, or an empty plastic milk jug with the top cut off and drain holes in the bottom.

Water the pecan when the dirt gets dry. If you are lucky, the pecan will sprout in the spring. If you have planted it in a container, wait until the winter before planting it outdoors.

You may have better luck if you buy a grafted pecan tree from a nursery. As you look for a tree, you will find that some different kinds of pecan trees have Native

American names— Choctaw, Caddo, Cheyenne, Pawnee, Shawnee, and Kiowa. Ask for help in choosing a tree that will grow well in your area.

Watch the young tree as it grows. Pick off any insects that start eating the leaves. Water the tree if the weather is dry. Pecan trees don't like "wet feet," but they do get thirsty sometimes.

Be patient. You will have to wait about seven years or more before your tree will start bearing pecans.

Pecan trees can grow tall. Some stand higher than a two-story house. They are fun to climb and make good places to hang a swing.

In the summer pecan trees make shade with their thick leaves. Shade helps a house stay cool and saves water in the grass.

By planting a pecan tree, you will help a true friend keep growing for everyone to enjoy. ▪

For more information about pecans, check the sources below.

◆ Bertline, Terry Scott. *Cooking with Pecans*. Austin: Eakin Press, 1986.

◆ Brison, Fred R. *Pecan Culture*. Texas Pecan Growers Association, Drawer CC, College Station, Texas 77840.

◆ Capps, Benjamin. *The Indians*. New York: Time-Life Books, 1973.

◆ Cotner, Robert C., "James Stephen Hogg," *Handbook of Texas*. Austin: The Texas State Historical Association, 1952.

◆ Earle, Olive L. with Michael Kantor. "Pecan," *Nuts*. New York: William Morrow, 1975.

◆ Evans, A.S., "Pecan Industry," *Handbook of Texas*. Austin: The Texas State Historical Association, 1952.

◆ Fowler, Gene. "The Texas Pecan," *Texas Highways*, December 1993.

◆ Haislet, John. "The Governor Hogg Pecan," *Famous Trees of Texas*. College Station, Texas: Texas Forest Service, 1970.

◆ Kaiser, Jo-Ann. "Pecan—the other hickory," *Wood & Wood Products*, October 1990.

◆ McEachern, George Ray and Larry A. Stein, *Planting and Establishing Pecan Trees* (brochure), College Station, Texas: Texas Agricultural Extension Service, 1986.

◆ McEachern, George Ray and Larry A. Stein, *Texas Pecan Handbook*, College Station, Texas: Extension Horticulture, 1993.

◆ Newcomb, W.W., Jr. *The Indians of Texas*. Austin: University of Texas Press, 1961.

◆ Olcott-Reid, Brenda. "Pecans," *Horticulture*, October 1990.

◆ "Pecan," *State Trees*. New York: William Morrow, 1973.

◆ Peacock, Howard, "Our State Tree, the Pecan," *Texas Highways*, February 1986.

◆ "Edmund E. Risien," *San Saba County History*, San Saba, Texas: San Saba County Historical Commission, 1993.

◆ Storey, J. Benton. "Pecans Go to the Moon," *Pecan Quarterly*, Vol. 5, No. 2, 1971.

◆ *Taste a True Native—Pecans* and *About Texas Pecans* (brochures), Department of Agriculture, P.O. Box 12847, Austin, TX 78711. (no date)

◆ Woolfolk, Margaret. "The Pecan: America's Favorite Nut," *Early American Life*, October 1990.

Acknowledgements

Thanks to *Texas Child Care* magazine, Texas Department of Human Services, for giving me the opportunity to write the article that gave rise to this book. Thanks to Elsie Millican, San Saba, for loaning photographs of her grandfather, E.E. Risien, and the San Saba school children, and to Martha Newkirk, San Saba, for the "Hully Gully Handful" game. Thanks to Jim and Sue Crump, Seguin, for information and enthusiasm; to Louise Parks and Diana Garza-Louis, Austin, for the recipes; and to John Lipe, Fredericksburg, for information about tree planting. Thanks to George Ray McEachern and J. Benton Storey, Texas A&M University, for reviewing the manuscript. Love and thanks to my parents, Louis and Frances Jaska, Ross, Texas, and to Joe and Eva Langham, Tyler, for nurturing my fondness for pecans.

Sincere appreciation to elementary school teachers—Michael Hamilton, Eanes Independent School District; Kathy Edwards, Hays Consolidated ISD; and Fran Richards, Dallas ISD—for reviewing a draft and photos.

Special thanks to the following for allowing photographs to be taken: Mary Ruth Wiley, Austin, pecans on her front yard tree; John and Dorothy Anderson, Seguin, harvesting at their orchard; Tom Vandivier and son, shelling operation at Navidad Farms, Austin: Austin Community Nursery School, children with nutcrackers; and Jim and Bonnie Hoekstra and their children at Garden Ville plant nursery, Austin.

Photo credits:

About the Author

Austin author Barbara A. Langham has developed educational materials used throughout the United States. She has written or edited several activity books for

preschool teachers, including *Room to Grow: How to Create Quality Early Childhood Environments*, and *Superbrush*, a preschool dental health curriculum. Since 1980, she has been a copy editor and regular contributor to *Texas Child Care*, a quarterly training journal.

Her articles on health, education, and history have appeared in *Texas Monthly*, *Texas Medicine*, and *Texas Highways*. She frequently writes on business topics for national trade journals.